make it in
Minutes

Greeting Cards

make it in Minutes
Greeting Cards

TAYLOR HAGERTY

LARK BOOKS

A Division of Sterling Publishing Co., Inc.
New York / London

Book Editor
Catherine Risling

Copy Editors
Lecia Monsen
Ana Maria Ventura

Photographer
Zachary Williams
Williams Visual
Ogden, UT

Stylist
Annie Hampton

Project Designers
Jennifer Barber
Lisa Gillis

Book Designer
Kehoe + Kehoe Design
Associates, Inc.
Burlington, VT

*Other Books
in This Series:*

Make it in Minutes:
Beaded Jewelry

Make it in Minutes:
Mini-Books

Make it in Minutes:
Mini-Boxes

Make it in Minutes:
Party Favors

A Red Lips 4 Courage Communications, Inc. book
www.redlips4courage.com
Eileen Cannon Paulin
President
Catherine Risling
Editorial Director

10 9 8 7 6 5 4 3

First Edition

Published by Lark Books, A Division of
Sterling Publishing Co., Inc.
387 Park Avenue South, New York, N.Y. 10016

Text © 2007, Taylor Hagerty
Photography © 2007, Lark Books
Illustrations © 2007, Lark Books

Distributed in Canada by Sterling Publishing,
c/o Canadian Manda Group, 165 Dufferin Street
Toronto, Ontario, Canada M6K 3H6

Distributed in the United Kingdom by GMC Distribution Services,
Castle Place, 166 High Street, Lewes, East Sussex, England BN7 1XU

Distributed in Australia by Capricorn Link (Australia) Pty Ltd.,
P.O. Box 704, Windsor, NSW 2756 Australia

If you have questions or comments about this book, please contact:
Lark Books
67 Broadway
Asheville, NC 28801
(828) 253-0467
Manufactured in China
All rights reserved

ISBN 13: 978-1-60059-033-7
ISBN 10: 1-60059-033-0

For information about custom editions, special sales, premium and corporate
purchases, please contact Sterling Special Sales Department at (800) 805-5489
or specialsales@sterlingpub.com.

"A gentle word, like summer rain, may
soothe some heart and banish pain.
What joy or sadness often springs
from just the simple little things."

—Willa Hoey

Contents

Introduction

Sending a greeting card to family and friends is a lovely tradition that dates back hundreds of years. The oldest known valentine was a poem written in 1415 by Charles, Duke of Orleans, from his prison cell to his wife.

As the idea of greeting cards grew, people found many occasions to send them, including holidays, birthdays, and just to say hello. The greeting card became a fixture and its popularity has continued to grow ever since. Nowadays it is possible to send a greeting in diverse ways, ranging from the traditional paper card to an electronic "e-card."

As the scrapbook and paper crafting industry continues to explode, there has been a movement back to making cards by hand to add a more personal touch. A handmade card is very special; it's a gift, a message, and a small work of art that expresses feelings for family and friends in a way that's sure to be treasured.

Once you have some simple techniques down, it's all in the details. Within minutes you can have a handmade card just as special as the recipient.

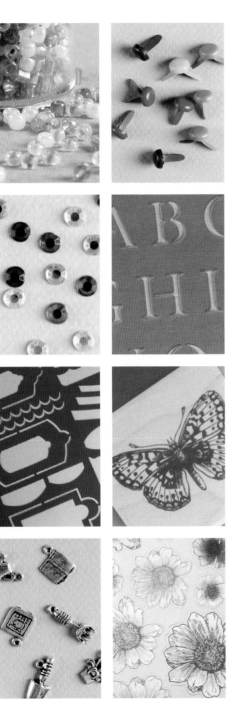

CHAPTER 1

Making a card begins with the correct paper. Most single-fold cards will require a more substantial 65-lb. cardstock, which is widely available in most craft stores as well as online. Cardstock is a stronger paper that can support multiple layers of embellishments, cuts cleanly, and works well when scored and folded or embossed. It is available in a wide range of colors, textures, and finishes. Many projects are well suited for 8½"x11" sheets but the 12"x12" size works well for creating several different sizes of square cards. Once you have chosen your card base, there are endless ways to embellish and personalize your designs for just about any occasion. This chapter introduces just a few of the numerous tools and techniques that will get you started.

Embellishments

Acrylic paint
A versatile medium, acrylic paint exists in an immense collection of colors and finishes. It can be used to paint an item or be watered down and used as a wash to age elements. It cleans up easily with water on brushes and skin, but is permanent on fabric, wood, and metal.

Beads
Beads add an elegant touch to a card. String them in a pleasing pattern on craft wire for a dimensional accent. Applying beads directly onto paper or cardstock requires the use of beading glue or tacky tape for a strong bond.

Brads
Available in a vast array of colors, shapes, and sizes, brads have a variety of uses from purely decorative to securing elements to a page. Some even have loops for stringing through ribbon or fibers, similar to lacing a shoe. To use a brad, simply poke a small hole in the paper, insert the brad, and open the prongs on the back to secure.

Buttons
With an almost limitless variety to choose from, buttons add a dimensional element to any design. Be sure to use glue dots, craft glue, a hot glue gun and glue sticks, or tacky tape for a strong bond.

Chalk
Chalks are used to create soft colors and shading using sponges, cotton balls, or swabs. This versatile medium can be used wet or dry.

Charms
These little ornaments add a pleasing dimensional touch to a card. Secure the charm to the design using glue dots, foam dots, craft glue, or a hot glue gun and glue sticks. If the recipient collects charms for a bracelet, present one as a gift by tying it onto the card using ribbon or wire.

Craft wire

Graphic and contemporary, craft wire makes a strong statement in card design. Typically used in beading, it also works well on its own as a closure or shaped into an abstract design. Adhere to project using glue dots, craft glue, or a hot glue gun and glue sticks.

Crystals

Crystals add a rich sparkle to a design. Be sure to use glue dots, craft glue, or tacky tape for a strong bond.

Die cuts

Die cuts add a dimensional element to a card when adhered with foam mounting dots or tape. They also work well to frame another component.

Fabric

Textiles are an excellent way to add depth and warmth to a card. Most patterned fabrics lend themselves well to photocopying to create custom papers for card designs. Adhere fabric using glue dots, foam mounting dots, craft glue, or a hot glue gun.

Glitter

There is a variety of glitter types in an enormous color palette available to embellish a card design. To ensure a solid bond, use tacky tape, glitter adhesive, or adhesive paper.

Paper

The primary element used in the creation of a card, paper is available in a wide variety of colors, types, weights, and textures. Paper can be adhered using practically any type of adhesive. When using vellum, vellum adhesive tape works best.

Polymer clay

Use this manmade clay to create an enormous variety of items to accent anything from paper crafts to clothing to jewelry. Keep clay clean while kneading and shaping by wearing latex gloves. This is particularly important when working with white or other light-colored clay.

Ribbon

Luxurious colors, sensuous textures, and a wide selection of sizes and styles make ribbons a beautiful touch on any card. The same adhesives used with fabrics work well for ribbons.

Rub-ons

These adhesive decals are applied to a flat surface using a craft stick. Available in numerous colors, images, fonts, and styles, rub-ons are a wonderful way to add a decorative touch to a card.

Silk flowers

Made from ribbon or fabric, silk flowers create a lovely dimensional look on a card, whether by using a single bloom or an entire garden. The same adhesives used with fabrics work well for silk flowers.

Stickers

Self-adhesive decals in a variety of styles, shapes, fonts, and sizes are used as embellishments or to form words for titling or journaling.

Yarn

The warm, organic nature of yarn offers a tactile element in card design. It can be used as an accent, similar to ribbon, or as a card closure. The same adhesives used with fabrics and ribbons work well for yarn.

Around the House

- Computer and printer
- Cosmetic sponges
- Cotton balls or swabs
- Pencils
- Sandpaper
- Scissors
- Stapler and staples
- Toothpicks

Adhesives

Acid-free adhesive dispenser

Adhesive application machine

Beading glue

Craft glue

Double-sided tape

Foam mounting dots

Foam mounting tape

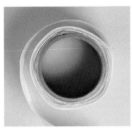

Glue dots

Glue stick

Hot glue sticks

Spray adhesive

Vellum adhesive tape

Tools

Bone folder

Colored pencils

Craft knife

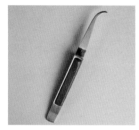

Craft tweezers

Crimping tool

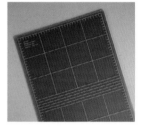

Cutting mat

Decorative-edge scissors

Embossing ink

Embossing powder

Embossing stencil

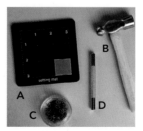

Eyelet-setting tools
A Setting mat
B Craft hammer
C Eyelets
D Eyelet setter

Foam brushes

Heat tool

Hole punch

Inkpad

Markers

Metal-edge ruler

Needle-nose pliers

Paper punch

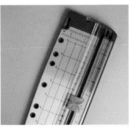

Paper trimmer

Piercing tool

Rubber stamps

Tag templates

Wire cutters

Techniques

Adhering crystals

Roll a small ball of beeswax and attach it to the end of a tooth-pick. Place a small amount of craft glue on a piece of card-board. Pick up a crystal by pressing the beeswax onto the top and then dip it lightly into the glue, wiping off excess on the cardboard. Place the crystal as desired and then remove it from the toothpick by pressing lightly on the crystal with your fingernail or tweezers; allow to dry.

Applying glitter

With slight pressure, glide craft or glitter glue bottle tip across paper to get the thinnest, smoothest, most intact line of adhesive as possible. Add more pressure to make different line widths. Using a spoon, sprinkle glitter on glue then tap off excess. It is important to apply the glitter to the glue while it is wet, white, and shiny, between 15–60 seconds. Glitter does not stick well to glue that has begun to dry.

Beading

Craft wire and jewelry wire, pliers, and beads are all readily available at craft stores. A few lovely beads in coordinating colors strung on a wire can embellish cards and add an interesting dimensional element. Strips of adhesive paper covered in seed beads can make a beautiful border accent.

Embossing

Embossing creates a raised effect on a stamped image. Stamp an image with clear embossing or pigmented ink then cover with embossing powder; tap off excess. Carefully wipe away any remaining embossing powder with a small, soft brush. Heat the powder using a heat tool until melted, forming a hard surface.

Rubber stamping

Basic stamping is an easy way to add flair to a card. Pat a stamp image firmly onto the surface of an inkpad. Position inked stamp above area to be stamped and press it firmly onto surface. Lift stamp off surface without smearing ink. Most permanent inks take a few seconds to dry. If needed, heat surface with a heat tool to set ink.

Polymer clay

This manmade clay is a satisfying way to add a three-dimensional touch to a design. The clay will not dry out when exposed to air for a long period of time. To permanently set a molded design, follow the manufacturer's directions to bake it in an oven. Once it has cooled, it can be painted and embellished.

Making a Card

Cutting: The basic tools for cutting cardstock or paper are a craft knife, paper trimmer, or scissors. Because of cardstock's thickness it is easier to obtain a clean cut using a paper trimmer or craft knife. Be sure it has a sharp blade.

Scoring: Once you've trimmed your chosen paper or cardstock to the size you want, you will need to score and fold the card. If you are using plain or decorative paper, you can simply fold the card and crease it with your finger. To get a nice, sharp fold using a thicker paper, try using a scoring tool and bone folder, which are sometimes the same tool. Cardstock will not fold cleanly without being scored first. With a change of the blade, a paper trimmer can also score cardstock.

To score your card, mark the top and bottom edges of the paper or cardstock where you want it to fold. Line a metal-edge ruler up on your marks, then firmly draw the scoring tool along the edge of the ruler. Fold the card over and, using the bone folder, press the crease down until it lies flat.

Making an Envelope

Materials

- Acid-free adhesive dispenser
- Paper
- Pencil
- Ruler
- Scissors
- Scoring tool

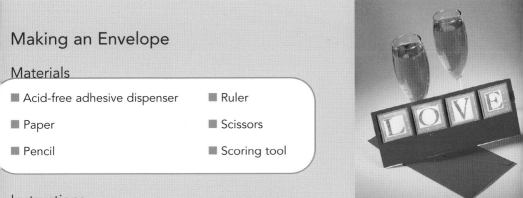

Instructions

1. Measure card front and add at least 1" to width for side flaps. Double card height and add at least ½" for top flap. Mark paper with these dimensions and cut out shape.

2. Score fold lines for top flap and envelope bottom. *Note:* These can be adjusted as long as the card's dimensions are retained for the front of the envelope. Trim top flap and envelope ½" in on either side to scored lines.

3. Fold envelope on scored lines. Unfold and apply adhesive on side flap backs. Refold, adhering flaps to inside back of envelope.

CHAPTER 2

Many times a purchased card doesn't quite express the thoughts and feelings you want to convey. Oftentimes, a handmade card will be treasured and kept long after the gift has been used up, worn out, or discarded. After all, you've created a small piece of artwork that is unique to the person who receives it. Commemorate that special day with a card designed specifically for the birthday person using his or her favorite colors, latest hobby, or a photo of the recipient, or design the entire card based on the sentiment. Choose a greeting that is humorous, serious, or meaningful to the two of you. Decide on the size of card and then select colors and embellishments that will complement the feeling you want to communicate.

Tiny Enclosure

Materials

- Acid-free adhesive dispenser
- Cardstock: green, lavender, pink, purple, yellow
- Craft knife
- Cutting mat
- Foam mounting dots
- Hole punch
- Paper punch: pom-pom
- Ribbon: yellow gingham
- Scissors

Instructions

1. Cut and fold pink cardstock to create 3"x 2½" side-fold card.

2. Adhere ribbon across front and back of card, leaving about 5" hanging off right sides of card.

3. Cut 2¾"x 2¼" piece of lavender cardstock; adhere to front of card.

4. Cut 2½"x 2" piece of purple cardstock. With craft knife, cut out birthday gift shape; adhere to front of card.

5. Cut birthday gift shape out of pink cardstock, slightly smaller than window in purple cardstock; adhere to front of card. Cut out green cardstock pieces to make "ribbon" and "bow"; adhere to front of card. Hole punch several purple dots; adhere to front of card.

6. Punch pom-pom shapes out of yellow cardstock; adhere to card using foam mounting dots.

7. Tie ribbon on side of card to close.

time-saving tip

Don't Make Just One

This card can easily be adapted for other occasions by changing the shapes and colors. Make several for the holidays or to have on hand for weddings or bridal showers.

Swirl & Ribbon

Materials

- Cardstock: pink
- Glue dots
- Ribbon: pink grosgrain
- Scissors
- Stickers: alphabet letters
- Wire spiral paper clip

Instructions

1. Cut and fold cardstock to create 3½"x 3" top-fold card.

2. Wrap ribbon through each side of wire spiral paper clip and around back of card front as shown in photograph; adhere ribbon in back with glue dots to secure.

3. Spell "Happy Birthday" with stickers.

time-saving tip

Choosing Alternate Elements

Substitute alphabet stamps, rub-ons, or your own handwriting for the stickers. Change the wire spiral to a ribbon slide or charm or use slide mounts to hold a vellum greeting and delete the words below. The wire spiral on the card could also hold a silk flower or "bouquet" of latex balloons that are ready for a party. The possibilities are endless!

Confetti Confection

Materials

- Acid-free adhesive dispenser
- Brads: gold (2)
- Cardstock: white
- Decorative paper
  (3 coordinating patterns)
- Foam mounting dots
- Hole punch
- Scissors
- Vellum sentiment

Instructions

1. Cut and fold cardstock to create 8½"x 5½" top-fold card.

2. Cut one strip of decorative paper to 8½"x 3"; adhere to front of card with acid-free adhesive dispenser.

3. Cut second strip of decorative paper to 8½"x 2"; adhere to front of card with acid-free adhesive dispenser.

4. Cut third strip of 5"x1¼" decorative paper. Trim vellum sentiment to fit on paper; punch two holes, then secure with brad on each side. Mount foam mounting dots to back; adhere to front of card.

time-saving tip

Printing Sentiments Ahead

Planning ahead is the key to a quick card. Print out and trim several different types of vellum sentiments so they will be ready when you need to make a quick card.

Happy Birthday to You

Materials

- Cardstock: blue, red, white
- Decorative paper
- Decorative-edge scissors
- Foam mounting dots: small
- Glue stick
- Inkpad: black
- Paint pens: gold, silver
- Rubber stamp: candle
- Scissors
- Scrap paper

Instructions

1. Cut 3¼"x 5¼" card from blue cardstock.

2. Glue 2¾"x ¾" piece of decorative paper to white cardstock and cut out.

3. Using silver paint pen, write "Happy Birthday to You" on decorative paper several times and add circles, dots, and squiggle lines. Attach to card using foam mounting dots.

4. Cut 1¾" square red cardstock with decorative-edge scissors. Add foam mounting dots to back; adhere to front of card. Using silver paint pen, add circles, dots, and squiggle lines.

5. Stamp candle onto white cardstock. Color in candle with silver paint pen. Using gold paint pen, color in "flame." Cut out and affix to pink square with foam mounting dots.

6. If desired, add decorative paper to envelope and paint circles, dots, and squiggle lines.

make a wish

Make a Wish

Materials

- Acid-free adhesive dispenser
- Birthday candle
- Butter knife
- Cardstock: blue, red
- Craft glue
- Decorative paper
- Decorative-edge scissors
- Foam mounting dots
- Mini muffin cup: red
- Paint pen: silver
- Polymer clay: blue, orange, red, white, yellow
- Scissors
- Spray clear gloss varnish
- Vellum adhesive
- Vellum sentiment

Instructions

1. Cut two 4"x 9¼" cards from blue cardstock; adhere together with acid-free adhesive dispenser.

2. Cut ¾"-wide piece of decorative paper to fit length of card; adhere to left side of card. Outline strip with paint pen.

3. Cut 3"x 2¼" piece of red cardstock using decorative-edge scissors; paint edges with paint pen. Adhere foam mounting dots and mount to card.

4. Cut vellum sentiment using decorative-edge scissors and adhere to red cardstock using vellum adhesive. Paint edges with paint pen.

5. Form cupcake out of clay. To make icing, form ball out of clay using butter knife to "smooth" out as you would if icing a cake. Form dots with colored clay and press into "frosting." Push candle down, on back of cupcake, and then remove before baking. Bake as directed.

6. Spray baked cupcake with clear varnish; allow to dry. Glue on mini muffin cup and replace candle. Glue to front of card.

32

Let's Celebrate

Materials

- Beads: clear seed
- Cardstock: pink, white
- Craft glue
- Decorative paper
- Decorative-edge scissors
- Foam mounting dots
- Glue dots
- Hole punch
- Paper punch: flower
- Pencil
- Ribbon: pink sheer
- Scallop-edge scissors
- Scissors
- Vellum adhesive
- Vellum sentiment

Instructions

1. Cut and fold white cardstock to create 5½"x 8½" side-fold card.

2. Draw three layers of cake on pink cardstock. Cut out and glue layers together.

3. Punch approximately 30 flowers out of white cardstock. Adhere first layer of flowers to cake as shown and use finger to press in center of next layer of flowers so petals "stand" up. Glue to cake and then glue beads to center of flowers.

4. Cut "platter" out of white cardstock using decorative-edge scissors. Cut piece of decorative paper slightly larger, then adhere platter on top; glue cake on top of platter.

5. To create "Let's Celebrate" embellishment, cut 3½"x 2½" rectangle of pink cardstock using decorative-edge scissors. Add foam mounting dots on back. Adhere vellum sentiment to decorative paper using vellum adhesive; cut slightly smaller than pink rectangle. Add glue dots and mount to pink rectangle.

6. Punch two holes in center of rectangle, then add ribbon; tie in knot and adhere to front of card.

Acrylic Present

Materials

- Acid-free adhesive dispenser
- Acrylic block: 1¾" x 2" self-adhesive
- Brads: lavender (4)
- Cardstock: pink
- Chalk: purple
- Decorative paper
- Ribbon: pink grosgrain
- Scissors

Instructions

1. Cut and fold cardstock to create 5½" x 4¼" top-fold card.

2. Trim decorative paper to 5¼" x 4"; adhere to front of card.

3. Wrap ribbon around front of card towards bottom. Adhere to inside of card front.

4. Rub purple chalk into grooves on acrylic design, then peel off protective coating that comes with acrylic block. *Note:* The color will only appear in the design.

5. Cut 1¾" x 2" piece of pink cardstock; attach to back of acrylic frame using brads then attach to card over ribbon with adhesive.

time-saving tip

Applying Chalks to Cards

There are many ways to apply chalks. Try using make-up applicators, cotton balls, or cotton swabs. Moisten the applicator to intensify the chalk color.

Birthday Shapes

Materials

- Acid-free adhesive dispenser
- Cardstock: bright colors of your choice
- Felt-tip pen: black
- Hole punches (2 sizes)
- Pencil
- Scissors
- Waxed linen thread: red

Instructions

1. Cut and fold cardstock to create 5½"x 4¼" top-fold card.

2. Cut rectangles out of coordinating cardstock. Write "Happy" on one piece and "Birthday" on the other; adhere to front of card.

3. Trace birthday shapes and squares on cardstock; cut out. Tie waxed linen thread around gift box; adhere all pieces to front of card.

4. Using different size hole punches, punch out brightly colored circles and use to embellish shapes; adhere to card.

time-saving tip

Dressing Up Card With Circles

Circles punched out of scrap cardstock will liven up any project. To apply them quickly, spread clear-drying glue over the project and attach the circles on top of the glue, then allow to dry.

CHAPTER 3

Tiny toes, delicate little fingers, and a cherubic mouth; the arrival of a new life is always an event worthy of celebration. Welcome a sweet little thing into the world with soft colors, tender words, and delicate details. The design, textures, and sentiment you choose will set the theme. Expressions of hope and faith in the future and an affectionate greeting convey a desire for a positive beginning and expectations of a full life. These cards are sure to be carefully stored in baby books to be treasured for years to come. Create a card that reflects a happy adoption or the birth of twins. Perhaps you know an experienced mom who would appreciate a humorous perspective on the impact of the newest little arrival or arrivals.

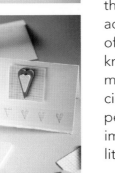

Sweet Boy

Materials

- Acid-free adhesive dispenser
- Brads: fish shape (3)
- Cardstock: blue, yellow
- Felt-tip pen: black
- Letter stickers: blue
- Paper punch: tag
- Ribbon: yellow
- Sandpaper
- Scissors

Instructions

1. Cut and fold blue cardstock to create 5"x 3" top-fold card.

2. Tear ½" strip off bottom front of card; distress inside bottom of card with sandpaper.

3. Punch three tags out of yellow cardstock; adhere letter stickers to spell out "boy."

4. Add fish brad at top of each tag; open prongs to secure. Glue ribbon across top front of card.

5. Adhere tags to front of card, overlapping ribbon as shown in photograph.

6. Write "sweet" on ribbon using pen.

time-saving tip

From Boy to Man

This card design can easily become a card for a man simply by changing the color of the cardstock and ribbon, the style of brads, and spelling D-A-D on the tags. If it's a card for the holidays, spell out J-O-Y and use appropriate colors and decorative brads.

Plaid Baby

Materials

- Acid-free adhesive dispenser
- Beads: alphabet, silver seed
- Brads: yellow (6)
- Cardstock: white
- Decorative paper
  (3 coordinating patterns)
- Dental floss: white
- Foam mounting dots
- Hole punch
- Scissors

Instructions

1. Cut and fold cardstock to 5"-square side-fold card. Cut and adhere decorative paper to front of card with acid-free adhesive dispenser.

2. Cut 2" square of white cardstock. Adhere coordinating decorative paper to cardstock with acid-free adhesive dispenser. Punch hole on left and right side of 2" square.

3. String alternating pattern of silver and alphabet beads on dental floss until desired word is complete. Thread ends through each hole and knot in back. Insert yellow brads in holes, then open prongs to secure.

4. Cut 3¼" square of white cardstock and punch holes in all four corners. Thread dental floss through corners and tie in back. Insert yellow brads in holes, then open prongs to secure.

5. Mount square with alphabet beads to 3¼" square with foam mounting dots; adhere to center of card with foam mounting dots.

time-saving tip

Personalize Your Cards

Spell out a child's name with stickers or rub-ons for an even more personalized card. Increase the cute quotient by using brads with decorative heads such as flowers, buttons, hearts, or stars. There are all kinds of clever brad styles available.

Just Ducky

Materials

- Acid-free adhesive dispenser
- Cardstock: blue, green, yellow
- Decorative-edge scissors
- Duck sticker
- Glue dots
- Paper punches: square (2 sizes)
- Ribbon: blue gingham
- Scissors

Instructions

1. Cut and fold yellow cardstock to create $3\frac{1}{2}$"x 8" side-fold card.

2. Cut green cardstock to $3\frac{1}{4}$"x $7\frac{3}{4}$".

3. Punch smaller square out of front of card yellow cardstock. Cut larger square out of green cardstock; adhere green cardstock to front of yellow card with acid-free adhesive dispenser.

4. Punch larger square out of blue cardstock; trim edges with decorative-edge scissors. Glue to inside of card so that waves are centered in square on front of card; attach duck sticker to center of square.

5. Attach piece of ribbon onto front of card with glue dots; tie bow and adhere.

time-saving tip

Getting the Bow Right

To make this easy bow, cut a length of ribbon and tie it into a bow. Cut another length of ribbon and adhere one end onto the inside of the card. Thread the ribbon through the die cut opening to the front of the card. Use a glue dot to secure the ribbon end to the card and attach the bow.

Baby Squares

Materials

- Acid-free adhesive dispenser
- Beads: silver seed
- Brads: star (4)
- Cardstock: blue, coral, green, pink, yellow
- Craft glue
- Fleece: white
- Foam brush
- Hole punch
- Paper punch: square
- Pinking shears
- Rubber stamps: alphabet letters
- Safety pins (4)
- Scissors

Instructions

1. Cut two pieces of coral cardstock to 9¼"x 3¾". Adhere together.

2. Punch four holes about ½" from card edge. Insert star brads in holes, then open prongs to secure.

3. Cut four squares from assorted cardstock. Apply craft glue to each alphabet stamp using foam brush. Stamp squares and apply silver beads immediately; allow to dry, then shake off excess beads. Repeat for each letter.

4. Using pinking shears, cut fleece squares about ¼" larger than cardstock squares. Glue each square to fleece.

5. Pin fleece with safety pins and hook around star brads.

time-saving tip

Giving Your Card Weight

If your design calls for one or more weighty embellishments on a single-fold card, reinforce the front panel with an additional layer of cardstock, which will stabilize the card.

Welcome Little One

Materials

- Acid-free adhesive dispenser
- Cardstock: pink
- Computer and printer
- Decorative paper: light colored
- Glue dots
- Ribbon rose embellishments
- Scissors

Instructions

1. Cut and fold cardstock to create 3"-square top-fold card.

2. Print "welcome little one" on light-colored paper; trim to 3"x 1" strip and tear edges.

3. Tear 1½" of bottom front of card as shown in photograph; adhere word strip to bottom inside of card.

4. Adhere ribbon rose embellishments to front of card using glue dots.

time-saving tip

Printing Text on Paper

To print text accurately from a computer onto patterned paper, type the desired text into a word processing program and print on plain paper. Trim the patterned paper to the size you desire. Center and tape the trimmed paper onto the computer paper on top of the printed text. Print the text document again while manually feeding the paper through the printer. This technique works well with tags and other small or oddly shaped papers.

Safety Pin

Materials

- Acid-free adhesive dispenser
- Cardstock: white
- Craft glue
- Decorative paper
  (2 coordinating patterns)
- Foam mounting dots
- Handmade paper
- Paper punch: square
- Ribbon: white
- Safety pin

Instructions

1. Cut and fold cardstock to create 4½"x 5½" side-fold card. Cut 5½" strip of handmade paper; tear edge and adhere to inside of card front.

2. Adhere coordinating decorative paper to front and inside of card with acid-free adhesive dispenser.

3. Punch square on front center of card.

4. Cut out rectangle a bit larger than safety pin; tie ribbon into bow around safety pin and then glue safety pin to rectangle. Mount entire embellishment to inside of card with foam mounting dots, centered in window.

time-saving tip

Using Different Charms

Use different embellishments such as a heart charm, bootie, or rattle in place of the safety pin to vary the look of the card. Make several of these sweet cards as a gift for the new mom to use as thank you notes.

Baby Letters

Materials

- Acid-free adhesive dispenser
- Acrylic paint: white
- Beaded chain: white
- Cardstock: blue
- Chipboard alphabet letters
- Decorative paper
- Foam brush
- Glue dots
- Ribbon: white grosgrain
- Scissors

Instructions

1. Cut and fold cardstock to create 7"x 5" top-fold card.

2. Trim decorative paper to 7"x 2". Tear bottom edge; adhere to top of card front using acid-free adhesive dispenser.

3. Tie knots in ribbon and weave beaded chain through knots.

4. Adhere ribbon across top front of card as shown in photograph.

5. Add color to alphabet letters using foam brush and acrylic paint; place letters on front of card using glue dots and weave beaded chain through "a."

time-saving tip

Adding Color & Sparkle

Add color to the die-cut letters using a foam brush and acrylic paints. Lightly wash each letter using watered-down paint and let dry. For a little extra sparkle, paint colored letters with craft glue and sprinkle on coordinating glitter.

Baby Girl

Materials

- Acid-free adhesive dispenser
- Acrylic paint: pink, white
- Craft glue
- Decorative paper
- Foam brush
- Foam mounting tape
- Handmade paper: white
- Paper punches: small heart, square
- Wooden hearts (1 large, 1 small)

Instructions

1. Cut and fold handmade paper to create 5"x 4" top-fold card. Tear bottom edge of front of card.

2. Paint large wooden heart pink and small wooden heart white; allow to dry.

3. Glue small heart to large heart; allow to dry.

4. Punch five hearts on front edge of card as shown in photograph. Adhere 1" strip of decorative paper to inside of card, where hearts are cut out.

5. Punch square out of white cardstock and decorative paper; adhere together.

6. Glue wooden hearts onto square; allow to dry.

7. Adhere foam mounting tape to back of square and mount on card front.

time-saving tip

Reinforcing Handmade Paper

Handmade paper is often very thin. To reinforce it, adhere it to cardstock for added stability. Choose a colored cardstock to coordinate with the paper. The color of the cardstock will affect the color of the paper somewhat so if it is important to stay true to the paper color, use white cardstock.

CHAPTER 4

These days, with all the hustle and bustle of modern living, keeping in touch with friends and family is difficult to do. Because we are all so busy with the daily challenges of living, it is a great pleasure to open the mailbox and find an unexpected note or card from a loved one. Immediately we feel a warmth for, and connection to, the sender. A lovingly crafted card speaks to your recipients, telling them how important they are to you because you spent time to make something special just for them. There is no limit to those who would enjoy a card telling them what their friendship means to you. There is something very special in a hand-written missive that an e-mail or phone call can't deliver.

Fun Friend

Materials

- Acid-free adhesive dispenser
- Brads: white (6)
- Cardstock: blue, white
- Decorative paper
- Glue dots
- Letter stickers
- Scissors
- Wood tags: white (3)

Instructions

1. Cut and fold blue cardstock to create 6"-square top-fold card.

2. Trim decorative paper to 2½"x 5" and adhere to right side of front of card.

3. Spell "Fun" on wood tags using stickers. Add white brad at top of each tag; then open prongs to secure. Attach to card using glue dots.

4. Spell "friend" on rectangular piece of white cardstock; adhere to front of card.

5. Attach three white brads in left corner of card, then open prongs to secure.

time-saving tip

Changing Colors

Change plain metal brads to match the color of your design. Simply rub the head of the brad in embossing ink, then sprinkle it with embossing powder in the desired color and heat with an embossing gun. Be sure to hold the powdered brad with craft tweezers while you melt the powder.

Girlfriend

Materials

- Acid-free adhesive dispenser
- Brass template: leaf, shoe
- Cardstock: cream, green, pink
- Computer and printer
- Embossing stylus
- Light table
- Sandpaper
- Scissors

Instructions

1. Cut and fold green cardstock to create 5"x 3½" top-fold card.

2. Distress edges of green card using sandpaper.

3. Cut cream cardstock to 4¼"x 2¾"; using computer, print "girlfriend" on cardstock, then adhere to front of card.

4. Using light table, stylus, and brass template, emboss shoe onto pink cardstock and leaf onto green; cut out leaf and shoe. Turn shoe and leaf over and run sandpaper over embossed ridges to distress, then adhere pieces to card front.

time-saving tip

Coloring Embossed Images

Once an image is embossed onto paper add color to the raised parts. Position the template on top of the raised image to act as a mask, and paint or chalk as desired.

You 'R' Fun

Materials

- Acid-free adhesive dispenser
- Alphabet stickers
- Cardstock: purple
- Cording: silver
- Decorative paper
- Fun sticker
- Ribbon: pink sheer
- Scissors
- Vellum tags

Instructions

1. Cut and fold cardstock to create 5"x 3" top-fold card.

2. Cut decorative paper to 5"x 1"; adhere to top front of card.

3. Place stickers on vellum tags, then tie ribbon onto each tag.

4. String tags onto silver cording, then tie cording around front of card.

time-saving tip

Printing Your Own Tags
Change the look of tags by printing letters from a computer on white or colored paper. Using punches the same size or shape as the tags, punch the shape out with the letters centered and adhere onto tag.

A Time to Remember

Materials

- Acid-free adhesive dispenser
- Cardstock: white
- Craft glue
- Craft wire
- Decorative paper: green patterned
- Foam mounting tape
- Ribbon: pink wire
- Scissors
- Silk leaves
- Vellum adhesive
- Vellum sentiment

Instructions

1. Adhere patterned paper to cardstock. Cut and fold cardstock to create 5"x 4¾" side-fold card.

2. Wrap ribbon around front of card; tie in bow.

3. Adhere vellum sentiment to 3"x 2½" piece of white cardstock using vellum adhesive; cut out. Add foam mounting tape on back; adhere to front of card.

4. Cut 8" length of ribbon and fold edge onto itself a few times, then fold ribbon in opposite direction to form rose petals. Repeat for remaining ribbon length and then wrap craft wire at base of flower to secure. Cut off excess craft wire and glue leaves to front of card. Glue flower on top.

time-saving tip

Changing Theme of a Card
The same card design can be used for many different themes. To alter this card's theme, simply choose a different vellum sentiment. Adapt an established design to the theme by using different colors and embellishments.

Floral Friend

Materials

- Acid-free adhesive dispenser
- Assorted beads
- Brads: flower (2)
- Cardstock: light blue, white
- Craft glue
- Decorative paper
  (2 coordinating patterns)
- Foam mounting dots
- Glue stick
- Hole punch
- Paint pen: gold
- Paper punches: flower
  (2 different sizes)
- Scissors

Instructions

1. Cut and fold white cardstock to create 4¾"-square side-fold card.

2. Cut and adhere decorative paper to front of card with acid-free adhesive dispenser.

3. Cut 1½" square out of light blue cardstock. Using gold pen, write desired sentiment.

4. Cover 2½" square of white cardstock with coordinating decorative paper using glue stick. Punch two holes at top corners. Insert flower brads, then open prongs to secure. Add foam mounting dots and attach to card.

5. Punch 14 large flowers out of decorative paper and 8 small flowers out of white cardstock. Glue first floral layer to card, then bend up petals on next two layers; glue in place. Glue beads to center of each flower; allow to dry.

6. Add foam mounting dots to back of light blue square; adhere on top of 2½" square. Glue final flower over "i" in "friend" and glue beads to center of flower.

time-saving tip

Making Flowers Stand Out
For a more contemporary look, use one patterned paper and one coordinating solid paper. Punch large flowers out of two different solid colors and the small flowers from the patterned paper.

Friendship Beads

Materials

- Beads: alphabet, green glass
- Cardstock: white
- Craft wire: 26-gauge
- Hot glue gun
- Paper punch: square
- Piercing tool
- Scissors
- Silk flower and stem
- Wire cutter

Instructions

1. Cut and fold white cardstock to create 3¾"x 6" side-fold card. Punch out front center of card using square punch.

2. Hot glue flower and stem into place; cut stem where card front meets open edge so card can open freely. Hot glue bottom of stem to front of card.

3. String green bead onto craft wire, then alphabet beads and a second green bead. Wrap each end of craft wire several times around piercing tool. Adhere ends of wire onto front of card over stem with dab of hot glue.

time-saving tip

Present Gift With Card

This is a great way to present your best girlfriend with a beautiful bracelet you've made or purchased. Punch a small hole on either side of the window and thread the end of the bracelet through each hole. Adhere ends to inside cover of card with cellophane tape for easy removal.

You Color My Life

Materials

- Acid-free adhesive dispenser
- Brads: silver (3)
- Cardstock: brown, various shades of blue, green, and pink
- Computer and printer
- Paper punches: square (4 graduated sizes)
- Piercing tool
- Scissors

Instructions

1. Cut and fold brown cardstock to create 7½"x 3½" top-fold card.

2. Trim piece of pink cardstock to 7½"x 1". Print words on pink cardstock using computer; adhere to bottom front of card.

3. Punch three squares each of three larger sizes using three shades of blue, green, and pink. Punch three small squares of brown cardstock.

4. Compile squares into little stacks and insert brad through middle of each one, then open prongs to secure. Adhere to front of card.

time-saving tip

Cutting Squares Quickly
If you do not have square paper punches, use a paper trimmer with a flip-out ruler attachment. Measure and cut each square using the ruler without making any pencil marks. Cut each set of squares ¼" smaller than the previous set.

Cheery Flowers

Materials

- Acid-free adhesive dispenser
- Cardstock: green, purple
- Decorative-edge scissors
- Embossing ink
- Embossing powder: white
- Heat tool
- Inkpad: purple
- Ribbon: purple with white flowers
- Rubber stamps: alphabet letters, flower
- Scissors

Instructions

1. Cut and fold purple cardstock to create 4¼"x 5½" top-fold card.

2. Using embossing ink, stamp flowers all over front of card. Emboss with white powder and heat tool.

3. Cut 4¼"x 1¾" strip of green cardstock with decorative-edge scissors; attach to front of card, layering with strip of purple cardstock and ribbon.

4. Stamp "Friends" on front of card.

time-saving tip

Using Patterned Ribbon & Stickers
Patterned ribbon can make a project come together quickly—instead of stamping an image, use stickers that coordinate with the ribbon.

CHAPTER 5

Writing a proper note of thanks is quickly becoming a lost art. Take a few moments to create a handmade card and fill it with a sincere note of appreciation. You'll be surprised at the response you get. Taking extra effort to acknowledge a friend's thoughtfulness and actions shows how much you appreciate what he or she did for you. A thank you card can be sophisticated and elegant, or simple and casual. Friends and family members are with us so often that we tend to take them and their contributions for granted. Be sure to thank them for simply loving and supporting you with a personalized note designed specifically for them.

Dragonfly Charm

Materials

- Beads: assorted
- Cardstock: blue, striped, white
- Charm: dragonfly
- Craft glue
- Craft wire: 26-gauge
- Foam mounting dots
- Glue stick
- Hole punch
- Inkpad: black
- Piercing tool
- Ribbon: white rickrack, white sheer
- Rubber stamps: alphabet letters
- Scissors
- Tag templates (3 sizes)

Instructions

1. Cut two large tags out of striped cardstock, one medium tag from blue cardstock, and one small tag from white cardstock.

2. Glue rickrack to front of large tag, wrapping ends around and gluing at back. Glue second large tag to back of first tag to hide rickrack edges; allow to dry. *Note:* The two layers will also make the card more stable.

3. Stamp desired sentiment on white tag; adhere to blue tag with foam mounting dots.

4. Pierce two holes at top of blue cardstock. Cut 3" length of white sheer ribbon; weave through holes, then tie loose knot.

5. String beads and charm onto craft wire. Thread one end of wire into ribbon knot and tighten knot. Wrap ends of craft wire around piercing tool to form "curled" craft wire ends.

6. Tuck blue tag in rickrack; secure in place with glue stick.

time-saving tip

Changing Your Charms

Completely change the look of this card by changing the charm or adding different beads to the finished project. Use a heart for love, a sunflower for friendship, or a cake for a birthday—the possibilities are limitless.

You Made My Day

Materials

- Acid-free adhesive dispenser
- Brad: white
- Cardstock: pink, white
- Craft glue
- Paper: pink
- Ribbon: white grosgrain
- Rub-ons: flower, mini alphabet letters
- Sandpaper
- Scissors

Instructions

1. Cut and fold white cardstock to create 6"x 2½" top-fold card.

2. Distress 5¾"x 2¼" piece of pink cardstock using sandpaper; adhere to front of card with acid-free adhesive dispenser.

3. Wrap ribbon around card front and adhere inside card with acid-free adhesive dispenser; rub words onto ribbon.

4. Rub flower onto scrap of pink paper, then cut out.

5. Insert brad through flower center, then open prongs to secure. Glue onto card.

time-saving tip

Distressing Your Cards
Different grains of sandpaper make different distressed looks.
For small areas or edges, use an emery board for greater control.

Flower Tag

Materials

- Acid-free adhesive dispenser
- Brad: pink
- Cardstock: pink, yellow
- Decorative paper: striped
- Mini rub-on letters
- Piercing tool
- Scissors
- Vellum tag: flower

Instructions

1. Cut and fold yellow cardstock to create 3½"x 8" side-fold card.

2. Cut striped paper to 3½"x 4¾"; adhere to bottom of card front.

3. Cut strip of pink cardstock to 3½"x 1"; adhere over top of striped paper.

4. Rub saying onto flower tag. Adhere to top of card front using brad, then open prongs to secure.

time-saving tip

Ready for Card Making

Plan ahead to be ready when creativity strikes. Rather than using stickers, stamp words and letters ahead of time and allow to dry. Cut them out while watching TV or talking on the phone. The greeting part of the card will be ready when it's time to make a card.

Floral Yarn

Materials

- Beads: clear seed
- Cardstock: green, white
- Craft glue
- Craft knife
- Cutting mat
- Embossed paper
- Felt-tip pen: black
- Foam mounting dots
- Paper crimper
- Scissors
- Vellum
- Vellum adhesive
- Yarn: green

Instructions

1. Cut and fold white cardstock to create 5"x 6½" side-fold card.

2. Cut out center of card front to form "window" using craft knife.

3. Crimp and cut out green cardstock to 5"x ½". Glue to front of card as shown, then glue on beads; allow to dry.

4. Write sentiment on vellum using black pen. Cut out and adhere to embossed paper using vellum adhesive; glue to white cardstock and cut out rectangle. Add foam mounting dots to back and adhere to card. Add beads as desired.

5. Cut 1" circle and ¼"-wide strip out of crimped cardstock. Form flower petals with yarn, gluing in place. Fill in each petal with more yarn and glue circle in place; adhere to center of card. Add dollop of glue in center of circle, then add clear beads; allow to dry.

6. Cut crimped cardstock strip to create "stem" and glue at base of flower.

time-saving tip

Adding Knitted Embellishments

To create a yarn design, try cutting shapes out of an old knit sweater. This is a great way to recycle a well-worn sweater or scarf. If you don't have a sweater or scarf, try using fleece or other material with distinctive texture.

Paper Flowers

Materials

- Acid-free adhesive dispenser
- Brads: green (5)
- Cardstock: white
- Computer and printer
- Craft glue
- Decorative paper
  (2 coordinating patterns)
- Foam mounting dots
- Hole punch
- Paper punches: flower
  (3 sizes)
- Pencil
- Piercing tool
- Ribbon: green
- Scissors
- Vellum
- Vellum adhesive

Instructions

1. Cut and fold cardstock to create $5\frac{1}{2}$"x $8\frac{1}{2}$" side-fold card.

2. Cut $2\frac{1}{2}$"x $8\frac{1}{2}$" strip of decorative paper and adhere down right side of front of card.

3. Punch flowers out of decorative paper and layer by size. Using piercing tool, curl up edges of flowers. Pierce holes through center of each flower and insert brads, then open prongs to secure. Glue onto front of card.

4. Cut 9" length of green ribbon, then knot it in several places, making bow at ends. Add craft glue just under flower; shape bow to form "leaf" and then glue in place. Glue tails in place; allow to dry.

5. Print sentiment on vellum. Adhere sentiment to $3\frac{1}{4}$"x $1\frac{1}{2}$" piece of coordinating decorative paper using vellum adhesive.

6. Cut white cardstock to $4\frac{1}{4}$"x 2"; adhere to back of sentiment.

7. Punch two holes on either side of vellum sentiment and insert green brads, then open prongs to secure. Mount onto front of card using foam mounting dots.

Springtime Sentiment

Materials

- Cardstock: white
- Craft glue
- Craft wire: 26-gauge
- Decorative paper
  (3 coordinating patterns)
- Decorative-edge scissors
- Foam mounting dots
- Hot glue gun
- Inkpad: green
- Piercing tool
- Ribbon: green sheer
- Rubber stamps: alphabet letters
- Scissors
- Silk flower

Instructions

1. Cut cardstock to 4"x 9" card.

2. Cut one 4"-square piece of decorative paper and glue onto front of card. Cut one 2" square out of coordinating paper. Cut one 3" square out of third coordinating paper using decorative-edge scissors; layer and adhere squares to front of card with foam mounting dots.

3. Wrap stem of silk flower with craft wire and bend as shown. Hot glue flower to front of card.

4. Pierce two holes at top of card, insert ribbon through holes, and tie knots at top.

5. Stamp "Thanks" on front of card.

time-saving tip

Working With Floral Stems

Wrap wire around the flower stem before shaping it to help it hold a more detailed shape. If you prefer not to have a curly stem, simply trim the stem off an inch or so below the flower.

Butterfly in Flight

Materials

- Acid-free adhesive dispenser
- Brads: black (4)
- Cardstock: black, white
- Computer and printer
- Decorative paper (3 coordinating patterns)
- Embossing heat tool
- Embossing powder
- Inkpad: pink
- Rubber stamp: butterfly
- Scissors
- Vellum
- Vellum adhesive

Instructions

1. Cut and fold black cardstock to create $3\frac{1}{2}$"x 8" side-fold card.

2. Cut three $3\frac{1}{4}$"x $2\frac{1}{2}$" pieces of decorative paper, then adhere to front of card using acid-free adhesive dispenser.

3. Cut 2" square of white cardstock and $2\frac{1}{4}$" square of black cardstock. Stamp butterfly on small square of white cardstock.

4. Stamp butterfly on piece of vellum. Sprinkle embossing powder on image, then heat with embossing heat tool; cut out.

5. Adhere body of vellum butterfly to top of cardstock butterfly so wings stick up using vellum adhesive; attach white square to black square using black brads, then open prongs to secure. Adhere to front of card.

6. Print "Thank You" on white cardstock. Cut out and adhere to front of card.

time-saving tip

Drying Ink on Vellum
Pigment ink stays wet when applied to vellum paper so you can use clear or sparkle embossing powder and emboss any color without special embossing ink. Be careful when using a heat tool with vellum so that it doesn't accidentally melt the paper.

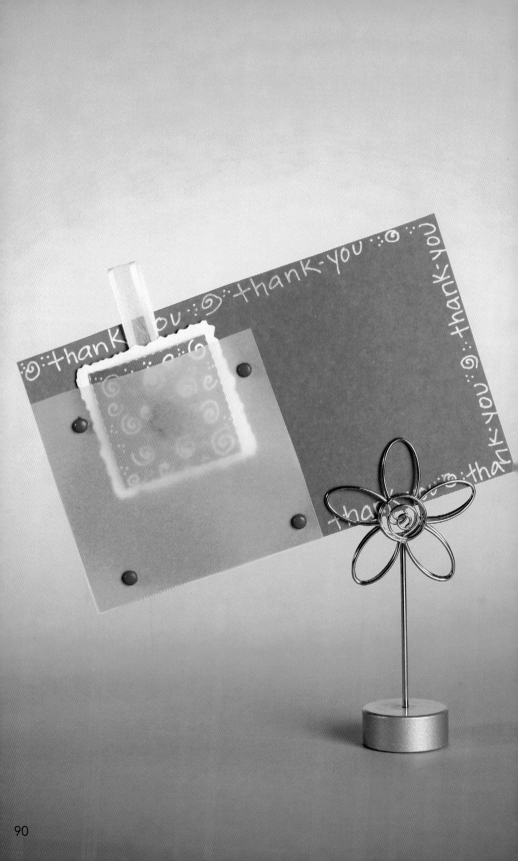

Flower Magnet

Materials

- Brads: pink (4), purple flower (1)
- Cardstock: pink, purple, white
- Craft glue
- Decorative-edge scissors
- Foam mounting tape
- Magnet sheet
- Paint pen: silver
- Piercing tool
- Ribbon: white
- Scissors
- Vellum
- Vellum adhesive

Instructions

1. Cut purple cardstock to 5½"x 3¼" to create card.

2. To make "magnet," cut two 2" squares of white cardstock using decorative-edge scissors. Loop 2" of white ribbon and "sandwich" ends between layers of white cardstock, gluing layers together. Cut magnet sheet to size and adhere to back of cardstock squares.

3. Cut one pink cardstock square slightly smaller than white squares. Make doodles and squiggles with silver paint pen; allow to dry. Pierce hole in center and insert purple brad, then open prongs to secure. Adhere to white square using foam mounting tape.

4. Cut square piece of vellum paper about 1" larger than cardstock magnet. Layer vellum square on top of cardstock and then pierce four holes in each corner. Insert pink brads, then open prongs to secure.

5. Write "thank you" on card and draw squiggles and dots using silver paint pen; allow to dry.

time-saving tip

Adding Magnetic Backings

Make the card a gift as well by adding magnetic dots to the back of the embellishment. Another easy way to add a magnetic backing is to use an adhesive application machine with a magnetic cartridge.

CHAPTER 6

During difficult times, an expression of support and empathy to someone suffering a loss is a lifeline for them to cling to. When that expression is featured on a handcrafted card created specially for them, your concern and sympathy are broadcast clearly. Whether in response to the loss of a friend, beloved family member, or pet, a sympathy card is a tangible symbol of your desire to comfort the recipient. Sometimes disappointments, such as not getting that new job, deserve concern and support too. Sympathy cards are generally composed of serene colors and sentiments but if the occasion and recipient merit a more colorful feel, choose colors, verses, and designs that are respectful of the circumstances.

Flower Bunches

Materials

- Acid-free adhesive dispenser
- Cardstock: seafoam
- Computer and printer
- Craft glue
- Inkpad: seafoam
- Paper: white
- Ribbon: sheer seafoam
- Scissors
- Silk flowers (3)
- Sponge

Instructions

1. Cut and fold cardstock to create 5"x 7" side-fold card.

2. Using computer, print sentiment onto $4\frac{3}{4}$"x $6\frac{3}{4}$" piece of paper.

3. Sponge ink all over paper to add color; adhere to front of card.

4. Tie ribbon around flowers and glue to front of card; allow to dry.

time-saving tip

Using Alternate Flowers
Instead of using silk flowers, use flowers made with paper punches, dried flowers, stickers, or rub-ons. The idea is to use what you have on hand so you can make your card in minutes.

So Sorry

Materials

- Acid-free adhesive dispenser
- Cardstock: cream, lavender, pink
- Fine-tip pen: black
- Paper punch: pom-pom
- Scissors
- Sequins

Instructions

1. Cut and fold cream cardstock to create 3"-square top-fold card.

2. Cut 1" from bottom edge of front of card. Punch pom-poms out of lavender cardstock; adhere along bottom edge.

3. Adhere sequins randomly to front of card.

4. Cut 3"x 1" strip of pink cardstock; adhere to inside bottom edge of card.

5. Write sentiment with black pen.

time-saving tip

Cards with Many Uses
Leave the sentiment off and these cards become a great gift enclosure. Make up several without a greeting to have on hand. You can add an appropriate title to the front as needed.

Thoughtful Tags

Materials

- Acid-free adhesive dispenser
- Cardstock: dark blue, light blue
- Computer and printer
- Mini safety pins: blue (3)
- Paper punches: tag (2 sizes)
- Ribbon: light blue grosgrain
- Sandpaper
- Scissors
- Vellum
- Vellum adhesive

Instructions

1. Cut and fold dark blue cardstock to create 3½"x 5½" top-fold card.

2. Distress front of card using sandpaper.

3. Print words on vellum paper using computer.

4. Punch out tag shapes from vellum paper so words you just printed are in desired location.

5. Punch bigger tag shapes out of light blue cardstock; tear edges.

6. Attach vellum tags to blue cardstock tags with vellum adhesive; attach ribbons using mini safety pins.

7. Adhere tags to front of card.

time-saving tip

Attaching Vellum to Cards

Use eyelets, brads, safety pins, or ribbons to attach vellum to prevent a regular adhesive from showing through. As an alternative, there are special vellum adhesives available on the market.

With Sympathy

Materials

- Beads: clear seed
- Cardstock: cream
- Craft glue
- Decorative paper: purple plaid
- Felt-tip pen: black

- Glue dots
- Paper punch: flower
- Ribbon: white
- Scissors

Instructions

1. Cut and fold cardstock to create 3½"x 5" side-fold card; tear right edge of card front.

2. Punch 18 flowers out of plaid paper; add glue dot to back of each flower and layer together, varying levels of flowers so some "pop" off the page more than others. Glue flowers to card.

3. Glue beads to center of each flower, then draw stems and leaves. Write desired sentiment.

4. Make bow out of white ribbon; adhere to front of card with glue dots.

5. If desired, add flower embellishments to envelope.

time-saving tip

Adding More Dimension
Add stronger dimension to this card by using foam dots behind the flowers and the bow. Instead of drawing the stems, use regular or waxed green floss.

You're in Our Thoughts

Materials

- Cardstock: blue, white
- Craft glue
- Craft knife
- Cutting mat
- Flower sprigs with stems and leaves
- Hole punch
- Paint pen: gold
- Ribbon: green satin
- Scissors
- Vellum: patterned
- Vellum adhesive

Instructions

1. Cut and fold white cardstock to create 5"x 6½" side-fold card. With craft knife, cut out center to create "window."

2. Bunch flower sprigs together and then wrap with craft-wire stems. Tie green satin bow around bunch.

3. Cut 3¼"x 5¼" piece of blue cardstock and glue centered to inside of card.

4. Cut and adhere vellum to fit entire inside of card using vellum adhesive.

5. Glue flower bunch to card; allow to dry completely.

6. Outline frame opening with paint pen and write desired sentiment.

time-saving tip

Saving Package Wrapping

Save silk flowers from packages or discount stores. Beautiful paper can also be kept and used later to embellish your own greeting card.

Thinking of You

Materials

- Acid-free adhesive dispenser
- Cardstock: white
- Craft glue
- Craft knife
- Cutting mat
- Decorative paper
- Felt-tip pen: black
- Ribbon flowers (3)
- Scissors

Instructions

1. Cut and fold white cardstock to create 6½"x 5" top-fold card. With craft knife, cut out center to create "window."

2. Cut and adhere decorative paper to inside of card with pattern showing through frame area.

3. Draw stems and leaves on front of card using black pen.

4. Glue ribbon flowers as shown in photograph; allow to dry.

5. Write desired sentiment on front of card.

time-saving tip

Adding a Sentiment Later
Make this an everyday card by not adding a sentiment. When you need a card, simply include whatever greeting suits the occasion.

thinking
of you

Floral Foldout

Materials

- Acid-free adhesive dispenser
- Computer and printer
- Decorative paper
  (2 coordinating patterns)
- Paper punches: square (2 sizes)
- Pencil
- Scissors

Instructions

1. Using pattern provided, cut card out of decorative paper; fold on fold lines.

2. Cut coordinating decorative paper and adhere to inside of card. *Note:* Adding a second sheet of decorative paper adds thickness and gives weight to the card.

3. Punch out and adhere larger square on left side of pullout.

4. Using computer and printer, print out sentiment on coordinating paper. Punch out smaller square and adhere onto larger square.

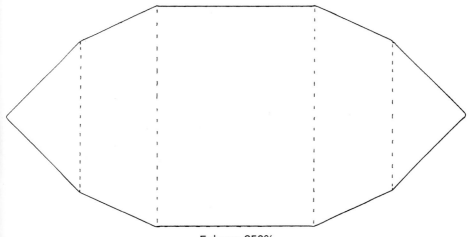

Enlarge 250%

Three Flowers

Materials

- Acid-free adhesive dispenser
- Cardstock: green, pink
- Decorative paper
- Glue dots
- Metallic paper
- Mini brads: pink (2), yellow (3)
- Paper punch: pom-pom
- Scissors
- Vellum
- Waxed linen thread: light green

Instructions

1. Cut and fold green cardstock to create $3\frac{1}{2}$"x $5\frac{1}{4}$" top-fold card.

2. Trim decorative paper to 3"x $4\frac{3}{4}$".

3. Trim metallic paper to $1\frac{1}{2}$"x 3".

4. Trim green cardstock to $1\frac{3}{4}$"x $3\frac{1}{4}$".

5. Layer and adhere papers to front of card.

6. Punch pom-poms out of pink cardstock and vellum; attach vellum to cardstock using yellow mini brads, then open prongs to secure.

7. Adhere piece of waxed linen thread onto back of each flower; attach to metallic paper using glue dots.

8. Attach layered strip of cardstock and decorative paper across card using pink brads, then open prongs to secure.

time-saving tip

Creating Flowers
While this card requires a flower punch, there are lots of shapes that will look like flowers when layered with vellum and given centers with brads, eyelets, or circle punches.

CHAPTER 7

Written expressions of love range from valentines and love letters to wedding congratulations and remembering anniversaries. Some are romantic in nature and others express love and affection. A young child, whether yours or a grandchild, niece, nephew, or special friend, will be thrilled to find a card telling of your affection and admiration for them in their backpack or pocket. Similarly, a note to a spouse or parent will warm the heart. Celebrate a wedding or anniversary with a custom-made card spotlighting that special day. Don't forget valentines for all your loved ones. There's a wistful second grader inside everyone, secretly hoping that he or she will receive a card from a favorite friend.

Embellished Silver

Materials

- Acid-free adhesive dispenser
- Cardstock: white
- Colored pencils
- Craft wire
- Decorative paper: silver
- Glue dots
- Hole punch
- Inkpad: permanent black
- Ribbon: silver
- Rubber stamp: bridal image
- Scissors
- Shrink paper

Instructions

1. Cut and fold cardstock to create 3½"-square top-fold card.

2. Cut 3¼" square out of decorative paper; adhere to front of card.

3. Stamp shrink paper using stamp and inkpad and color with pencils; cut out image.

4. Punch two holes near top of image. Shrink paper in oven or use embossing gun, following manufacturer's instructions.

5. String wire through holes, then tie ribbon around wire.

6. Attach image and ribbon to card front with glue dots.

time-saving tip

Adhering Shrink Plastic

Elements made from shrink plastic are hard to adhere using craft glue. Be sure to punch holes in the design before shrinking it and use ribbon, floss, or wire to attach it to the card. If it must be glued, roughen the back of the plastic with sandpaper and use strong-hold glue. Allow to dry completely.

Three Cakes

Materials

- Brads: pink (2)
- Cardstock: white
- Chalk: pink
- Cotton swab
- Cutting mat
- Embossing ink
- Embossing powder: silver
- Embossing stylus
- Foam mounting tape
- Rubber stamp: cake
- Scissors
- Sheet metal

Instructions

1. Cut and fold cardstock to create 7"x 5" top-fold card.

2. Stamp image all over card front using embossing ink; emboss with silver powder.

3. Shade parts of stamped image using chalk and cotton swab.

4. Cut sheet metal into three 1½" squares. Stamp image on back of squares.
   Note: Any kind of ink is fine as you won't see it on the finished product.

5. Set metal square on cutting mat, with stamped image face up. Trace stamped image using embossing stylus.

6. Turn metal squares over; attach squares together using brads, then open prongs to secure. *Note:* Brads will go in easier if you use a straight pin or piercing tool to make a hole where you want the brad to go.

7. Attach metal squares to front of card using foam mounting tape.

time-saving tip

Filling in Small Areas
Use the small end of the embossing stylus to fill in hard-to-reach areas or patterns of the design.

Ribbons & Hearts

Materials

- Acid-free adhesive dispenser
- Brads: baby blue (6)
- Cardstock: pink, white
- Paper punches: heart, square (2 sizes)
- Piercing tool
- Ribbon: red grosgrain
- Scissors
- Stipple brush
- Watercolors: red, white

Instructions

1. Cut and fold cardstock to create 6"-square side-fold card.

2. Using stipple brush and red and white watercolors, brush color on front of card. Make "x" mark numerous times with brush.

3. Punch square out of card front with larger square punch.

4. Cut 3" square out of pink cardstock; punch smaller square in center. Adhere to inside of card front, centering square cutouts.

5. Tie three lengths of ribbon into knots and attach to brads. Pierce holes at bottom of card and insert brads, then open prongs to secure.

6. Punch hearts out of pink cardstock; adhere to inside of card.

time-saving tip

Piercing Holes for Brads

Brads are easier to insert into projects if you use a pushpin or piercing tool to make a pilot hole first. This is especially important when using mini brads. A hole punch makes a hole that is too large and won't hold the brad securely.

Scallop Heart

Materials

- Acid-free adhesive dispenser
- Brad: heart
- Cardstock: pink, white
- Craft wire: 26-gauge
- Decorative paper: pink swirls
- Decorative-edge scissors
- Foam mounting dots
- Paint pen: silver
- Piercing tool
- Scissors
- Wire cutters

Instructions

1. Adhere decorative paper to pink cardstock with acid-free adhesive dispenser.

2. Cut and fold pink cardstock to 5½"x 4" top-fold card. Cut into heart shape using decorative-edge scissors.

3. Cut 1½" square white cardstock with decorative–edge scissors. With ends of piercing tool, poke two holes in each corner of square.

4. Cut 8" piece of craft wire; thread ends of craft wire into each hole and twist craft wire around piercing tool. Continue as desired and finish at other end.

5. Using silver paint pen, write desired sentiment.

6. Pierce hole in center of cardstock and add heart brad; open prongs to secure.

7. Adhere foam mounting dots to back of embellishment, then secure to front of card.

time-saving tip

Having Card Bases on Hand

The fastest way to make a card is to have one already done. Instead of making a single card at a time, make three or four to have on hand.

Gold Heart

Materials

- Acid-free adhesive dispenser
- Cardstock: cream
- Handmade paper
  (2 coordinating colors)
- Heart charm
- Ribbon: gold
- Scissors

Instructions

1. Cut and fold cardstock to create 4½"x 3" top-fold card.

2. Tear handmade paper to 4¾"x 3¼" and adhere to front of card with acid-free adhesive dispenser.

3. Tear 1½" square of coordinating handmade paper; adhere to center of card.

4. Tie gold ribbon and adhere to top of square.

5. Adhere gold heart in center of square.

time-saving tip

Tearing Edges of Paper
To tear handmade and mulberry papers more easily, trace a line on the paper where you want it to tear using a damp finger or a cotton swab dipped in water. This will give the paper a softer, more organic edge.

Forever in LOVE

Materials

- Acid-free adhesive dispenser
- Acrylic paint: red
- Cardstock: red, white
- Decorative paper: pink
- Foam brush
- Foam mounting dots
- Glue stick
- Paper punch: square
- Ribbon: red grosgrain
- Rubber stamps: alphabet letters
- Scissors
- Vellum: patterned
- Vellum adhesive

Instructions

1. Cut two 9¼"x 4"pieces of red cardstock.

2. Adhere 18" piece of grosgrain ribbon to front of one card with glue stick and allow to dry. Glue remaining ends to back of card and allow to dry.

3. Adhere second piece of cardstock to back of cardstock with grosgrain ribbon with acid-free adhesive dispenser.

4. Stamp each letter on white cardstock using red paint; allow to dry. Cut out, forming square shapes.

5. Punch four squares of patterned vellum and adhere letter squares to each using vellum adhesive. *Note:* Vellum should be slightly larger than alphabet squares.

6. Punch four squares of decorative paper and adhere to letters. Add foam mounting dot to back of each square; adhere squares on top of ribbon.

7. If desired, punch square in top corner of envelope to allow "L" to show through.

Wedding Cake

Materials

- Acid-free adhesive dispenser
- Cardstock: navy blue, white
- Craft glue
- Decorative paper
- Foam mounting dots
- Glitter
- Glitter glue
- Glue stick
- Paper punch: square
- Polymer clay: white
- Scissors
- Vellum adhesive
- Vellum sentiment

Instructions

1. Cut and fold white cardstock to create 8½"x 5½" top-fold card.

2. To make cake, form three "layers," largest on the bottom, with thin ropes and circles of polymer clay. Bake as directed by manufacturer; allow to cool.

3. Cut and adhere decorative paper to front of card with acid-free adhesive dispenser.

4. Punch square at top of card front. Using glitter glue, apply glue around opening and sprinkle glitter on top; tap off excess.

5. Lightly coat cake with glitter glue and sprinkle on glitter; tap off excess. Glue cake to 2" square of navy blue cardstock using craft glue; allow to dry. Add foam mounting dots to back of cardstock and adhere to inside of card.

6. Cut 3¼"x 2" piece of white cardstock. Apply glitter glue to edges, then sprinkle on glitter; tap off excess. Adhere foam mounting dots to back. Glue vellum sentiment (cut slightly smaller than glittered cardstock) to scrap paper using vellum adhesive; adhere to cardstock.

7. Center sentiment below cake on front of card and secure in place with glue stick.

May every day be a
celebration of the heart

Celebration of Heart

Materials

- Beads: silver seed
- Buttons
- Cardstock: red, white
- Craft glue
- Craft knife
- Cutting mat
- Foam mounting dots
- Paint pen: silver
- Scissors
- Vellum adhesive
- Vellum sentiment

Instructions

1. Cut and fold white cardstock to create 5"x 6½" side-fold card. Cut out center of card front to make "frame" area using craft knife. Draw heart using paint pen, then glue buttons and beads in heart area.

2. Adhere vellum sentiment to red cardstock using vellum adhesive; cut out to form rectangle. Add foam mounting dots to back of cardstock; adhere to front of card.

3. Glue buttons to front corners and glue silver beads on top of buttons; allow to dry.

time-saving tip

Working with Leafing Pens
Silver and gold paint or leafing pens are a great way to outline and highlight an area of interest on a card. Be aware that the pens are permanent, so consider the design carefully before committing to it on the card. If necessary, practice the design on some scrap paper first.

METRIC EQUIVALENCY CHARTS

inches to millimeters and centimeters
(mm-millimeters, cm-centimeters)

inches	mm	cm	inches	cm	inches	cm
⅛	3	0.3	9	22.9	30	76.2
¼	6	0.6	10	25.4	31	78.7
½	13	1.3	12	30.5	33	83.8
⅝	16	1.6	13	33.0	34	86.4
¾	19	1.9	14	35.6	35	88.9
⅞	22	2.2	15	38.1	36	91.4
1	25	2.5	16	40.6	37	94.0
1¼	32	3.2	17	43.2	38	96.5
1½	38	3.8	18	45.7	39	99.1
1¾	44	4.4	19	48.3	40	101.6
2	51	5.1	20	50.8	41	104.1
2½	64	6.4	21	53.3	42	106.7
3	76	7.6	22	55.9	43	109.2
3½	89	8.9	23	58.4	44	111.8
4	102	10.2	24	61.0	45	114.3
4½	114	11.4	25	63.5	46	116.8
5	127	12.7	26	66.0	47	119.4
6	152	15.2	27	68.6	48	121.9
7	178	17.8	28	71.1	49	124.5
8	203	20.3	29	73.7	50	127.0

yards to meters

yards	meters	yards	meters	yards	meters	yards	meters	yards	meters
⅛	0.11	2⅛	1.94	4⅛	3.77	6⅛	5.60	8⅛	7.43
¼	0.23	2¼	2.06	4¼	3.89	6¼	5.72	8¼	7.54
⅜	0.34	2⅜	2.17	4⅜	4.00	6⅜	5.83	8⅜	7.66
½	0.46	2½	2.29	4½	4.11	6½	5.94	8½	7.77
⅝	0.57	2⅝	2.40	4⅝	4.23	6⅝	6.06	8⅝	7.89
¾	0.69	2¾	2.51	4¾	4.34	6¾	6.17	8¾	8.00
⅞	0.80	2⅞	2.63	4⅞	4.46	6⅞	6.29	8⅞	8.12
1	0.91	3	2.74	5	4.57	7	6.40	9	8.23
1⅛	1.03	3⅛	2.86	5⅛	4.69	7⅛	6.52	9⅛	8.34
1¼	1.14	3¼	2.97	5¼	4.80	7¼	6.63	9¼	8.46
1⅜	1.26	3⅜	3.09	5⅜	4.91	7⅜	6.74	9⅜	8.57
1½	1.37	3½	3.20	5½	5.03	7½	6.86	9½	8.69
1⅝	1.49	3⅝	3.31	5⅝	5.14	7⅝	6.97	9⅝	8.80
1¾	1.60	3¾	3.43	5¾	5.26	7¾	7.09	9¾	8.92
1⅞	1.71	3⅞	3.54	5⅞	5.37	7⅞	7.20	9⅞	9.03
2	1.83	4	3.66	6	5.49	8	7.32	10	9.14

INDEX